BY

SUSAN A. LEBRON

ABOVE
BOARD
GROUP

Published by Above Board Group
DBA No Fig Leaves Allowed!
Chula Vista, CA 91914

For Wholesale Purchases, contact us at:
author@nofigleaves.com

Retail Purchases can be made through various outlets or directly from Above Board Group at:
WWW.NOFIGLEAVES.COM

LIBRARY OF CONGRESS CATALOGING-IN-PUBLICATION DATA
LeBron, Susan A., author
No Fig Leaves Allowed! / Susan A. LeBron
p. cm
Includes bibliographical references and index
ISBN: 978-0-692-27106-3 (trade paper)
1. Relationships 2. Communication 3. LeBron, Susan A
WWW.NOFIGLEAVES.COM

Scripture quotations taken from The King James Version, KJV.
Copyright 1977, 1984, 2001 by Thomas Nelson, Inc.

Cartoonist: Jennifer Hodges
Cover Designer: Lori Star
Edited and Typeset by Bookmarq.net

Printed in the United States of America on Acid Free Paper

No Fig Leaves Allowed!

Thank you to . . .

. . . my husband; for allowing me to reflect on my past, explore my emotions and feelings, our marriage, and my connection with family and friends for the past eighteen years of "for better or worse." I thank you for *"Getting Naked!"* with me. I appreciate your being willing to listen to the wind and adjust your sails.

. . . my children; their eyes of truth and raw honesty see the good in me and the parts of me that still need work. You continue teaching me so much about life and true unconditional love. You are all incredible gifts to me. You came into this world Naked and I hope you stay that way.

. . . my mother; for climbing the mountain of forgiveness with me as our tears flowed in love during blunt and often very painful recollections of my childhood and life decisions. I thank you for supporting my efforts to break the cycle and "stay-on-the-wall".

. . . my extended family; for sowing the seeds of honesty through countless discussions and emotional brawls in the hopes of reaping more truthful and enduring relationships.

. . . to my Naked friends and neighbors; a very special thanks for your moral support, for keeping me grounded; for all the business and legal advice, and, oh yes, for serving as the voice of reason when I went off on my many dream-stream tangents.

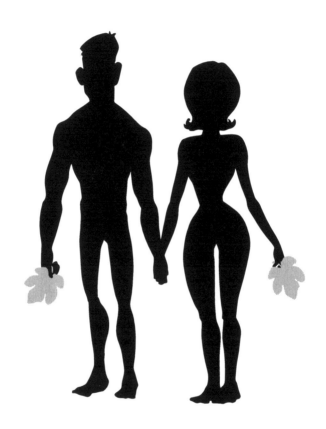

This book is nakedly dedicated
to my sister, Lisa.

What's in Here

No Fig Leaves Allowed!

Before you *"Get Naked!"*, Stop!!!

This guide is for educational purposes only and not intended to replace professional counseling. If you are currently experiencing emotional or physical abuse or have experienced abuse, loss, or other trauma in your life, please seek professional help.

To successfully achieve true emotional nakedness for the purpose of deeply connecting in a relationship, participants must willingly tackle tough topics, deep emotions, and both real and perceived vulnerabilities they might rather avoid.

Warning: In pursuing emotional nakedness, the truths revealed might unearth tremendous hurts or shatter the image participants have been hiding behind – perhaps for years. It is possible that in the quest of honest communication the viability of the relationship explored may be either confirmed or exposed to doubt.

The intent of this guide is to make you aware of your true self, your needs, and your expectations. *The "No Fig Leaves Allowed!" Approach* aims to help you strengthen your relationship through honest communication. *It is not intended to replace professional counseling.*

§

Once emotional nakedness is achieved, the question is whether or not you want to move your relationship in a positive direction. Are you willing to address the issues emerging out of this process and make the changes needed to nurture the honest and emotionally intimate relationship you seek and deserve?

If you answered 'yes' to the previous question, then commit to engaging in open, loving, honest, and mutually respectful communication with your partner. Commit to honoring, strengthening, and preserving your treasured relationship.

Your first step: Take a moment to reflect on the state of the relationship you seek to examine. Where are you now? Where do you want to be? What do you expect to accomplish in reading this book? What do you want to get out of applying *The "No Fig Leaves Allowed!" Approach*. Write your thoughts down. We'll come back to them later.

A note to the reader: "He" and "She" are used interchangeably throughout this book. The concepts explored here are equally applicable across genders and nothing should be construed to be exclusive of one or the other. However, where gender specificity is required, it is explicitly stated.

My Story

A fter years of allowing others to decide my value, I felt used and fed up with dating. I had grown intolerant of casual relationships. I needed something deeper. Why couldn't my suitors be honest and express what they wanted up front? Why the games? I grew weary of being led on for weeks and months thinking one fellow or another was "THE ONE" to complete me, just to be disappointed time and again. I was tired of being shown only the side of them they thought would lead to a sexual conquest. Sure, there were a few sensitive types in the mix, but I didn't see a future with any of them. After kissing my share of frogs, I learned Prince Charming was an elusive and emotionally unavailable joke. I stopped dating.

The workplace was no different. I found it a house full of mirrors where no matter how many projects I successfully completed or accolades I earned, there was always a one-upper who had to shine brighter; truth be damned.

Ever the optimist, I kept plugging along and focusing on me. At twenty-six, I decided I needed a change. I left my fun job traveling the country teaching postal exam workshops and took on a new career in corporate training and development. I decided to take on a new attitude as well. I worked hard and found joy in the little things. I liked myself and absolutely loved my work. I began to be 100% honest with myself, and with others, about how I felt. I began interacting with people using honesty and candor. It really worked and it weeded out the riff-raff. Life was goooood. It was about to get better.

One late mid-September night in 1996 I was out with friends

at a popular Orlando, Florida Salsa dance-club. From across the dance floor I spotted this flirtatious glance from a guy I deemed not too bad looking. I flashed a smile and fluttered my fingers at him to let him know I had caught him in his stare. In a short while, with cool confidence and in a gentlemanly manner, he made a bold move and asked my dance partner for permission to dance with me. Doing something like that in a hot-blooded Latino environment could have started a mucho-macho cock-fight. Fortunately for him, my dance partner and I were not "involved." I went on to dance the rest of the night with this tall Puerto Rican Mambo King.

OK, so he wasn't Fred Astaire on his toes that night, but he was tall, dressed smartly, had a strong lead, and was articulate with every word. Everything about him projected prince, not frog. I was curious. Before he left, he asked if he could call me. I thought, "why not?" We exchanged numbers and that was the end of the night.

He called the next morning and asked me to lunch. We met for what turned out to be a three-hour "interview." *Well, he didn't know it was going to be an interview. He just wanted a lunch date.*

I was just days from turning twenty-seven and had run the gauntlet of dates and mistakes (more on that in my next book). I wasn't about to waste any more time on empty chat and soulless sexual advances. I could take myself out to dinner and a movie if I wanted. I did not need a man; I *wanted* a partner and a family. I *needed* to put all of my desires out on the table on that very first date. Why waste time? I had all I needed in my life and was ready to share it with someone special. I was not interested in casual dating. My life was good and more focused now than ever before. The difference was my *wanting* someone to share it with instead of my *needing* someone to "complete me."

My date didn't know it yet, but I had my own haunted past. I was a child of twice divorced parents, spent years sowing wild oats while searching for that elusive "Prince," endured the trials of teen pregnancy, and on and on. Things were looking up, however. Though not quite where I wanted to be professionally, I had finished my Bachelor's Degree in Behavioral Studies and had a budding career as a corporate trainer. After wandering the desert of hopeless relationships, I finally valued myself enough to demand the relationship I deserved. As I subjected my date to some hard questions and hardline demands on our first outing together, I thought to myself, "If he could handle it, great. If not, fine." I was content to wait and continue working on myself.

As the hours passed and the chips and salsa were refilled again and again at my favorite Mexican restaurant, I thought for sure that my 'laying it out' on the first date would scare this man away. I was OK with that, but, to my surprise, apparently so was he. He neither shied away nor ran away. This was no frog. Years later, he admitted he thought my approach to our first date was as bold as it was refreshing. He said he appreciated meeting a woman who knew what she wanted and expressed what she needed. **By sharing what we thought was important in a relationship we eliminated the need to second-guess or read minds. We connected and decided we were made for each other right then and there.**

Our time together during courtship was fairly limited to meals. Our schedules would only allow time for lunch and dinner during the week and a few hours on weekends. Even so, we made the most of our limited time. We talked about everything. The romance came with opening doors, poems, love letters, and flowers left on my car's windshield almost every morning. This was quite something since he lived and worked on the other side of town. He courted me sweetly as our attraction grew. I admit there was no love early on, but I was impressed. Our respect, appreciation, and admiration for each other grew quickly as we accommodated the steep learning curve of our blossoming relationship. Things moved fast. To my surprise, just one month after our lunch date, he proposed. I said, "Yes. Emphatically yes!"

We set a date and six months after our first dance I married my Puerto Rican Mambo King.

The months leading to the wedding were a whirlwind. We both worked full-time and over-time as we planned our big day. We attended counseling meetings with my pastor and participated in a pre-marital "Engaged" Encounter weekend. Some days the tension would get to us and we would argue all the way to our counseling sessions. Once there, however, we would share what we liked or admired about each other and would focus back on what mattered most; our relationship.

Through this process we both realized our individual pasts affected our present. We also learned we both carried some emotional baggage we needed to release. What we didn't realize, was that the future would not only bring challenges to us as individuals but also to us as a couple. You see, almost immediately we began to change.

In the nine short months after the wedding our lives changed dramatically. I left my job and lost my figure to pregnancy, we left my family and moved to the snowy North East, and I gave birth to our son. My new husband was a naval officer and, other than thinking how AMAZING he looked in his uniform, I had no idea what I was getting into. Along with taking care of an infant, going to playgroups, cleaning the house, and cooking my husband's favorite meals, I was also taking on yet another new role as a military spouse.

I expended every bit of myself trying to be the perfect Navy wife – not easy to do when I had never been exposed to military life. This new role meant volunteering, attending spouse meetings, and entertaining. It meant long days apart and short nights together. It meant family separations and emotional reunions. It meant a life subordinated to the needs of my husband. My whole world had changed.

Meanwhile, my husband was focused on what he thought was the best way to show he loved me; he went to work and paid the bills. But the pressure of being a new dad and being the sole provider for the three of us proved a heavy toll on him. He didn't want to come home and be reminded of the added pressure so he lengthened his hours at work. I felt alone and neglected. I thought, "What about me and my needs?" I felt empty and unable to give of myself any longer. I didn't feel emotionally safe. We were quickly becoming sterile roommates. Where were the love notes? Was there any love left? Was this just a mistake? This was not equitable. Not fair! Did he change his mind about wanting to be married or just wanting me? Was he really a frog after all? I felt I had gotten the ole' bait & switch. The wall of resentment went up, leaving all chance of intimacy out in the cold. We couldn't communicate. We had hit the mute button. Sometimes I felt I wanted to hit the eject button too. I'm sure he would say the same. I am glad we didn't.

This frustrating scenario has played out several times over the years. With each transfer, birth of a child (six of them to date), deployment, moves, health challenges, weight fluctuations, or new demands on our time and talents, came new trials. With each trial came the need to refocus on each other. Each time we began to drift apart we talked and fought our way back from the brink of marital collapse. We decided we *did* want to be married and make our family work. Though we lacked the tools for effective communication early on, we shared a mutual commitment to each other and to our family. So we *fought* for our family – and we *fought hard for it*. I've always said, *"You don't fight for something you don't want."*

Some topics were painful and others were less so. If subjects were too hot to handle verbally we would use a journal in an effort to find a solution. We don't use the journal anymore. In applying the principles of *The "No Fig Leaves Allowed!" Approach*, we developed a mutually satisfying and loving sanctuary where feelings can be shared without risk of attack or blame. By focusing on truths, facts, and each other, we created our Safe Haven and our path to enduring intimacy. He feels safe to share feelings and concerns and I feel safe to open up my own emotions, express my needs, and "turn down the bed covers," — *wink, wink.*

You and your partner must create a Safe Haven for each other in your relationship. This is very important to the health of the partnership and can also be a huge adjustment for those of us accustomed to and comfortable with keeping the peace or the status quo. My husband and I were committed to nurturing a healthy marriage. For us, emotional nakedness evolved over the course of a decade. After nineteen years together, we still *Get Naked!* I'm not telling you it will take ten years for your relationship to flourish; but it could. It took us that long to get the hang of integrating this approach to communication in every exchange because we were learning as went along – as most people do. Don't give up. It's worth it. But now that I know *The "No Fig Leaves Allowed!" Approach* works, I can share it with you and perhaps help you get emotionally naked in your "Safe Haven" too.

As my husband and I understand all too well, employing *The "No Fig Leaves Allowed!" Approach* doesn't mean you won't have disagreements or face off in heated debates. Believe me, WE DO! What it means, however, is that you now have a way to freely give and receive of your hearts and hurts without risk and with confidence, because you both know you are committed to 100% honesty, 100% of the time. Being "all in" in any relationship you value is going to take an effort. Marriage certainly brings its own challenges and is not for sissies!

> "*Marriage is not for sissies*"

The "No Fig Leaves Allowed!" Approach helped me strengthen relationships with other people too. My relationship with my mother and stepfather, for example, has come a long way. We now say what's on our minds knowing we only want the best for each other. We know it all comes from the heart and is delivered with respect and pure intentions. Not everyone is ready to make the leap into honesty though. If some people in your life are neither ready nor willing to get emotionally naked, interactions with them will be superficial and strained at best, or irreparably broken, at worst.

You can't expect everyone to think exactly as you think and you shouldn't go along just to get along if it goes against your principles or your own good judgment. The key is to understand and be honest with yourself first. Don't compromise your values or miss opportunities to love, share, or experience life and relationships due to your own fears or shame. *The "No Fig Leaves Allowed!" Approach* helps you attain this understanding and self-awareness.

It Takes Two to Mambo . . .

I've been hurt by some people very close to me. Using *The "No Fig Leaves Allowed!" Approach* I shared my honest thoughts, feelings, and reactions with them. Some of those relationships ended while others endured only to become stronger. I believe that unhealthy and dysfunctional aspects of a relationship may have to die before being reborn into something beautiful. With communication and patience this is possible even with the same person.

This is not without the challenges of human emotions and requires commitment of both partners. It takes two to mambo.

When the time comes for you to *Get Naked*, do it. What others do is their business. Those decisions are theirs to make. You must, however, decide for yourself if you want the negativity to continue flowing into your own life. Only you can determine if having people, clad in Fig Leaves, in your life is worth enduring the constant strain. You can only do your part – you cannot also do theirs. Meanwhile, you can focus on and enjoy the good in

Getting Emotionally Naked!

your life, take off your own fig leaves, and set a positive example for others including your partner to follow.

Our Naked Family . . .

Children are notorious for telling it like it is. They are born "naked". They lack the filter and inhibitions we tend to develop as we age and begin molding our responses to fit what we think they should be. With kids, you can usually tell how they are feeling and when they are not happy. It is not until they start to get a bit older and begin to experience influences from friends, television, the Internet, and advertising, that many of them tend to become inhibited. This is also the time when they begin to form who they want to be as an individual, and start to assert themselves, which can create a great divide.

As our first three kids hit the pre-adolescence years, from nine to eleven, we noticed a change in how they related to each other, their friends, and to us. While there are age appropriate boundaries and vocabulary, my husband and I have taught, and continue to remind our children to take off their Fig Leaves. We encourage them to use *The "No Fig Leaves Allowed!" Approach* with us, and each other.

We have found that consistency with this approach helps keep the importance of communication a core value in our family. It's can be a delicate balance, but our experience has shown over time, at least in our family's case, it works. Our children communicate openly and freely about everything and are able to listen and accept loving correction. *The "No Fig Leaves Allowed!" Approach* has even helped me effectively communicate with my teenagers! That's a miracle in itself because we all know they speak a totally different language altogether! Whether it has been discussion on choices, responsibility, or about that "special" friend that seems to have red flags, (or fig leaves) which give us reason to pause.

Be Honest, Open, and True . . .

Through the process of removing my own Fig Leaves, I have found the majority of people like theirs just fine. Some sport them as if on a fashion runway while others wear them more modestly. Nevertheless, it's nearly impossible to build a real and emotionally naked relationship with a fake person. Maybe if you knew the real person you wouldn't want to build a relationship in the first place. Perhaps the relationship would be that much stronger if founded on truth. Maybe they know that, maybe they don't. But you know who you are and the relationship you deserve. Be honest, open, and true. Demand the same.

It's time to get real, people . . .

No Fig Leaves Allowed!

Get Naked!

Ground Rules

Though the Discovery Exercises in this book are not designed to incite a fight, it is possible you will face some emotional challenges as information is exchanged and feelings are shared along the way. This is normal. Keep your cool — and view upsetting feedback objectively and calmly, not as personal attacks. Learn to be proactive and effective in your communications. *Remember, a relationship is not a competition, it's a collaboration.*

Rules for Discussions and Debates

1. "No Fig Leaves Allowed!"

This phrase will serve as the seal on your covenant for effective communication. When one of you seems reluctant to move forward or gets defensive while sharing feelings or thoughts, firmly, but in love, say, *"No Fig Leaves Allowed!"* to remind each other you dwell in a Safe Haven in your discussion.

2. Keep the Safety On!

Arguments, hurt feelings, disagreements, and ruffled feathers are inevitable. Don't allow the "yucks" to stretch on indefinitely. If you must table a discussion, do so, but make an effort to regain the intimacy and fun of your relationship.

Think of a funny word or phrase, a handshake or shimmy, to cue each other that all will be calm even if you still have issues pending. Keyword examples include things like the place where you first met, the name of your first dance song, the name of someone you both admire, your children's names, or an obscure word you either make up or look up in the dictionary.

Make a list of your own cues now as a concrete reminder that the decision to do so was made ahead of time and framed by rational thought. If these are established ahead of time it will eliminate, or at least mitigate, flippant and inflammatory remarks such as my personal non-favorite: *"I'm done talking."* Words like these only serve to fuel-the-fire on the path to emotional scorched-earth.

Although a topic may be too hot to touch at the moment, a tabled discussion is just that, tabled. You eventually have to come back to it and resolve it. Individually reflect on whatever issue is holding you back. Decide on a time and place to talk about it, and then talk about it. Resolve it in love and with compassion. Don't let it fester indefinitely. It will come back and haunt you.

3. No Right or Wrong

Each time you come to an impasse there is potential for the discussion to lead to hurt feelings. As you listen to the content of the message always be sure to consider the intent. Ask yourself questions like: *"Does this person intend to hurt me?"* or *"Is she trying to wound my spirit or simply hold me accountable?"* or *"Am I upset because I am being asked to remove a Fig Leaf I am not ready to take off?"*

Understand that adopting *The "No Fig Leaves Allowed!" Approach* to communication is a process. It may take more time to perfect for some than others. It took us a decade to get it right! Patience and commitment are key. If you truly want this effort to be effective, forcing the issue is not the way to get your partner to reveal elusive inner feelings. You could potentially cause him or her to have an even firmer grip on his or her leaves.

If you are the one sharing, be aware of your intent. Ask yourself questions like: *"Am I trying to help my partner understand my feelings or issues or am I trying to make a point, defend myself, or prove just how wrong he really is?"*

Keep in mind there is no right or wrong, only feelings that need to be understood. Don't take things personally. Work towards *"a better us."* Choose *"we"* over *"me"* and *focus on strengthening your relationship*. Truly committed couples can weather almost any storm. Though you may have to adjust your language or your delivery, if you are truly committed, the chances are your relationship will be stronger as a result.

4. Make, and take notes

Though you need to keep focused on the current activity or topic, you may have a revelation about an earlier exercise while working on another. Jot all your thoughts in the note-sections or in a separate notebook. Without prior agreement, note-taking can seem rude and confrontational, so talk it through beforehand outlining that the only purpose of it is to provide an *aide-mémoire* and a true record of your discussions. Ensure you agree to share notes and discuss them later.

One of my (many) faults is I tend to speak out and respond when my husband is sharing. It drives him nuts when I "interrupt" his flow in an effort to make my own comments. It can be tough to sit and listen patiently — especially when you believe you are being misunderstood and want to respond before you forget. Note-taking can mitigate the outburst since you can write down reactions and address them later without the chance of forgetting. Try to adjust the way you take notes to fit your own needs. As long as you both understand the rules, note-taking and taking turns can work very well towards increasing information transfer. Be patient, these new behaviors may take time to sink in.

5. Be honest and descriptive

When answering questions, write down your initial thoughts. Do not overthink, rationalize, or filter your answers. Give details — with examples if possible — as you share your feelings. If you can relate-to or empathize with your partner by citing a previous experience, you should say so. Whether you draw a mental picture or a stick figure on paper to explain how you feel and how you understand, *it is important to let each other know that the message sent was the message received.* This effort builds confidence and understanding.

Creating Your Mutual Safe-Haven

This guide is intended to help you create and cue a Mutual Safe-Haven for sharing. When you take off your Fig Leaves and establish emotional nakedness, you should feel free to be honest with yourself and share openly with your partner. Your Mutual Safe-Haven should be a special place where you can be 100% honest with each other — with minimal risk of unrealistic expectations and misunderstandings. Your relationship will benefit from the more effective and open communication that removing your Fig Leaves and *"Getting Naked!"* brings to it.

Bonus: *Should you decide to consult a professional counselor your completed guide may also be used as a resource to pinpoint issues for follow-up to further sort out your feelings.*

YOUR NOTES

No Fig Leaves Allowed!

Why We Cover Up . . .
. . . and, Why A Fig Leaf?

Who we are – or who we have become – is a function of many things: genetics, the environment, family structure, schooling, and expectations. We need to acknowledge these influences and focus on understanding the tendencies that lead us to bite vigorously into the temptations – or as I prefer it "apples" – that society places in front of us.

Apples? . . . What Apples?

A short drive, a few minutes in front of a television or conversations with peers will reveal evidence of the continuous bombardment of unrealistic expectations aimed at shaping how we look, act, and feel. With all of these "pop culture" apples falling on us and telling us what "sexy" is, what "love has to do with it" and what makes a family, defines what we, or the world around us perceives as beautiful, or how a perfect relationship works.

"Don't bite into the hype"

We are bombarded with seemingly juicy and tasty apples all the time. They represent the notorious "Forbidden Fruit" which we all bite into in an effort to "fit-in" and be what others think we should be.

Considering how we have bitten into (and bought into) these "pop culture" apples and have been persuaded to eat them core-

and-all, it's no surprise how many people come to have a negative self-image. It's common to feel as if we fall short of who we think we want to be, or should be when we compare ourselves to a billboard image, a picture in a magazine or a star on a screen.

Believe me, you don't have to bite into the hype.

Consider how these apples can create a domino effect and demoralize even the most self-confident person who does not conform to what is presented as "perfection":

Her Apples: "I am not beautiful unless I know Victoria's Secret, have a rockin' body and salon hair, and am ready & willing to have sex on a whim. I must bring home some bacon and fry it up as I bake cookies for the PTA, all while cleaning the house and kissing the kiddies goodnight."

His Apples: "I'm not built like Adonis; I don't look like Brad Pitt; I don't make enough money and don't drive the cool car. My bank account is too small and my belly's too big. Oh, and I need a membership to Hair Club for Men!"

Let's Analyze This:

Pick any one of the following:

- I don't think I am attractive to my husband or wife;

- My partner's reaction to me isn't what it was in the beginning of our relationship;

- I am overweight and don't wear trendy clothes or make-up. My body isn't what it used to be;

- I never finished school. I don't contribute or make enough. I'm just so tired and feel guilty because I can't seem to be all I think my partner needs me to be; and

- How can my partner fulfil my needs when I can never be what my partner needs me to be?"

Fear: "He has or will lose interest in me and fantasize about other women, eventually cheating on me; *or* I know she looks at other men and wishes I was like them."

Potential Behaviors: One pulls away from the other. The weight piles on as insecurities mushroom. Depression grows and dependency spikes. Partners become anxious. Communication stalls. Paranoia and indifference set in. Talk becomes self-deprecating. Sex without emotional investment is sought.

Result: Partner and family pull away. Relationships become shallow, aggressive, and distant. Intimacy and communication evaporate. Relationships potentially end as partners go numb and lose faith that anything they say is well received. Some go on to surrender to the attention and affection of others as they engage in affairs of the body, heart, or mind. Fig Leaves are worn. The relationship fails.

Now, Let's Upset The Apple Cart . . .

Regardless of where the apples come from the insecurities they spawn can be addressed or remedied by taking action, realigning self-expectations, sharing feelings, or simply asking for help.

Make no mistake, the insecurities are very real and weigh heavily on the heart, the mind, and ultimately on the relationship. Conversely, though a partner may see the one he loves beyond the extra pounds or frazzle, the persistent boo-hooing, self-deprecation, and rejection of love advances eventually become grating and can grow into intimacy and communication issues. This can seem like a hopeless cycle. That type of relationship would seem one to run from for sure.

However, partners who have committed to each other have a responsibility to work through their insecurities and understand the cause of pain as they honor their commitment to making it work.

Use this next segment to put your apples into the right context. Acknowledge the apples' impact on your life. Let them serve not as poisons to your souls, but rather as fruits for motivation to accept that you are unique and beautiful individuals of high self-worth. We need not measure up to others' expectations; it is to our own naked self-expectations to which we must measure up.

So tip the apple cart: Take this opportunity as a time of personal discovery to unload your apples.

Getting to the Core . . .

Examples of some common apples we bite into:

- **You're not sexy enough.** Your partner works with several attractive people you feel have "perfect" bodies. You feel threatened and allow your body image to put distance between you two in the bedroom.

- **You're 30, 40, or 50 and should be married.**

- **You are divorced and not in a rush to commit** but feel that since you've been dating your current partner for months now and your friends are all paired up you should "settle down" again.

- **Achievement disappointments.** Your partner has advanced degrees and a successful career. He often talks about the success of people he admires. You chose to put

No Fig Leaves Allowed!

your career on hold to raise children. You feel inadequate because your skills have faded. You don't think you communicate on the same level or have anything in common. You feel put down, inferior, and maybe a bit jealous.

- **Keeping up appearances.** Your neighbors and friends have all the latest gadgets, tools, cars, and computers. You have chosen to be thrifty with your finances but feel you should buy something extravagant to show you can afford the same lifestyle.

- **You are the "Perfect" couple.** Being seen as the "it" couple is flattering but it also generates a lot of pressure. To avoid judgment you may feel it difficult to admit you have a problem in your relationship. You suffer in silence. You feel no love at all.

Discovery 1:
How 'bout Them Apples?

There's a difference between being ambitious or pursuing genuine pleasure and putting on a phony visage for the sake of proving something to the world. The former represents healthy goals; the latter is a poisonous apple.

What apples have you bitten into that now have a bitter taste? What are some areas in your personal life you feel particularly pressured to perform in beyond your current capabilities, means, or emotional state? How about within your relationship? Write them down:

My Apples:

My Partner's Apples:

And now the Fig Leaves . . .

The Fig Leaf analogy is borrowed from the Bible's Book of Genesis. It refers to the notion that Adam and Eve had nothing to physically, emotionally, mentally, or spiritually to hide from. They were not *embarrassed* or *ashamed* in each other's presence, at least not until they bit into that apple. After their first nibble, their eyes were opened to their nakedness, but it wasn't their nakedness they covered with fig leaves; it was their shame.

Being naked wasn't wrong; being unfaithful was.

In this guide, the Fig Leaf symbolizes all the efforts we make to cover up the insecurities, unrealistic expectations, fears, and barriers that often lead to unsatisfying and stagnant relationships. The hope is that in removing your Fig Leaves, you can tackle the emotions and past hurts that serve as barriers to the relationship you deserve. The desire is for you to remove your shame so you can be emotionally, physically, mentally, and spiritually naked in your relationship as appropriate.

We are all at risk . . .

Not even considering the negative forces that tend to tear couples apart, even the most seemingly solid relationships can fall victim to the grind. Couples today are kept very busy with positive things in life such as work, kids, activities, friends, and maybe even some self-interested pursuits like working out, participating in sports, or even going to school.

But as couples get busier, they tend to adjust to and accept a lower standard of communication and intimacy just to make it day by day. Their positive endeavors can turn into negative distractions if allowed to become the focus of living. Couples in this gridlock of modern living might feel it is easier to just go along to get along instead of fighting for a gratifying relationship. They get up, go to work, take kids to school, do their daily business, go home, eat dinner, get kids to bed, go to bed, and wake up to do it all over again the next day. Life is busy, but it's good enough. Or is it?

The *"No Fig Leaves Allowed!"* Approach is predicated on the notion that **good isn't good enough**. Simply getting along is not good enough and over time can leave one or both parties in a relationship feeling lonely and unfulfilled. Those feelings are often accompanied by thoughts of "what if," "maybe," "I wish he would . . . ," "why don't you . . . ," "she doesn't . . . ," and on and on. You both deserve better!

"Good isn't good enough"

A relationship is a give and take between two people who have committed to journey through part of life together. Though partners may get along fairly well, partners can't read each other's minds. Desires must be expressed, feelings must be shared if a couple is to understand each other's wants or needs. If a couple does not, cannot, or will not communicate openly about how they feel or what they need there will be trouble in paradise.

Fig Leaves do the most damage when they are consciously or subconsciously used as a coping mechanism to cover up vulnerabilities or create images of social or relational infallibility. In some cases, they may serve as insulation to disguise the boredom in the bedroom or the insecurities we feel about ourselves.

Whether our insecurities are real or imagined, our Fig Leaves prevent our true needs from ever becoming known or fulfilled. How can anyone expect to be well loved if there is an unwillingness to share what is needed to feel loved? How can anyone heal if not willing to accept they have been wounded or are unable to communicate their pain? How can anyone be expected to know

No Fig Leaves Allowed!

what is not revealed to them? That is simply not fair. It's not fair to your partner and it's not fair to you.

The discovery exercises in this book have been designed to help participants learn about each other. One of the most effective ways to learn something thoroughly is to teach it to someone else. Using *The "No Fig Leaves Allowed!" Approach*, you are going to teach your partner about yourself. Along the way, you might be surprised to learn a great deal about yourself too. The intent is to expose shames and remove Fig Leaves that often serve to cover, rationalize, or disguise feelings of inadequacy, inhibitions, false perceptions, and past experiences, all of which can squash any hope of an intimate relationship and personal peace.

Throughout this journey you will be provided with questions and phrases to elicit thinking and encourage evaluation of deep feelings on a variety of topics. Single participants can also apply *The "No Fig Leaves Allowed!" Approach* to enhance self-awareness. Being honest and open with yourself and others will be conducive to building both personal and intimate relationships in the future. It is incredibly liberating and empowering to be able to share everything early on and discover factors that may help determine the ultimate and long-term viability of a relationship.

For couples, these exercises will explore the quality of the relationship and perhaps reveal Fig Leaves best removed in the interest of intimacy. The sharing portion might seem more challenging than some of the other activities. If you and your partner embrace the activities and commit to using *The "No Fig Leaves Allowed!" Approach* daily you should be able to move forward together with a renewed commitment and create your own Safe Haven for honest communication.

Take a moment to think about the type of relationship you are striving for: How comfortable are you taking off your Fig Leaves and pursuing the kind of relationship you truly deserve? Do you have any reservations?

No Fig Leaves Allowed!

DISCOVERY 2:
THE COMFORT METER™

Losing Your Inhibitions

I t is possible to feel a high level of discomfort when posed with questions that peer deeper into parts of your soul not normally revealed. It is important to capture your first reactions to the questions presented on the following pages and to be 100% honest in how you answer. Remember, you must be mentally prepared to share openly and you must keep your relationship goals in the forefront of your thoughts. This commitment to open communication is central and crucial to your success in adopting *The "No Fig Leaves Allowed!" Approach.*

Your first discovery tool is the **Comfort Meter™**. It incorporates a comfort ranking system from **zero to four**. The purpose of this exercise is to provide you a tangible measure of how open you are in communicating with your partner and to enlighten you as to when and where in the discovery effort you need to tread with extra compassion towards the sensitivities of your partner.

If you are working this alone, you can also benefit greatly from the process. Through it you can learn useful information to help you discover what areas are especially sensitive for you so you can begin to understand why you may react strongly in some situations or discussions. Oftentimes, I have found that when my husband or I seem determined to not budge on an issue, it typically has to do with one or more of the areas you will explore on the next couple of pages.

Once a sensitive area is identified, continue on the thread to see if you can uncover the root of an emotional response. Usually, something from the past is influencing your response and it may or may not have anything to do with the issue at hand. Your effort to isolate the cause of your response and separate it from your current discussion will help you make reasonable and logical decisions on how to resolve a clash of wills.

Open and honest dissection of the Comfort Meter topics encourage participants to move a relationship in a positive direction, by developing their communication skills. The process is like walking into a dark room in fear, only to turn on the lights and discover there is nothing there that can harm you. Before the switch is flipped, however, you must feel your way around obstacles until you figure out what they are and where you need to go. Some obstacles you can move totally out of the way while others you may have to learn to maneuver around together. Don't worry – if you work together, you will find that switch.

Directions:

Read each discussion topic and rank from zero to four. Zero indicates you do not feel comfortable with the topic at all and would rather not share anything about the issue. Four indicates you welcome discussion, are completely comfortable sharing and you have no inhibitions about the issue at all.

Your answers will provide critical insights as you evaluate your ability and willingness to communicate with each other. The ultimate goal is to get to a point where most – if not all – topics can be discussed openly. Hold on to your answers. We will revisit them further along.

# The Comfort Meter (Self)
0= No Way; 1= Maybe; 2= OK; 3= Yes; 4= Emphatically Yes!

Hot Topic	0	1	2	3	4
Being Naked					
Feelings					
Trust					
Faithfulness/Infidelity					
Communication Quality					
Career/Career Choices					
Finances					
How You Spend Money					
How Your Partner Spends Money					
Children					
Parenting/Discipline					
Your Relationship					
Past Relationships					
Sexual Satisfaction					
Sexual Health					
Relationship Counseling					
Mother					
Father					
Siblings					
Partner's Family					
Body					
Partner's Body					
Health					
Partner's Health					
Educational Level					
Partner's Educational Level					
Having Fun					
Fitness/Exercise					
Church/Religion					
What's Important To You					
How Your Partner Makes You Feel					
Whether Or Not You Feel Valued					
The Future					

No Fig Leaves Allowed!

# The Comfort Meter (Partner)
0= No Way; 1= Maybe; 2= OK; 3= Yes; 4= Emphatically Yes!

Hot Topic	0	1	2	3	4
Being Naked					
Feelings					
Trust					
Faithfulness/Infidelity					
Communication Quality					
Career/Career Choices					
Finances					
How You Spend Money					
How Your Partner Spends Money					
Children					
Parenting/Discipline					
Your Relationship					
Past Relationships					
Sexual Satisfaction					
Sexual Health					
Relationship Counseling					
Mother					
Father					
Siblings					
Partner's Family					
Body					
Partner's Body					
Health					
Partner's Health					
Educational Level					
Partner's Educational Level					
Having Fun					
Fitness/Exercise					
Church/Religion					
What's Important To You					
How Your Partner Makes You Feel					
Whether Or Not You Feel Valued					
The Future					

No Fig Leaves Allowed!

S.H.A.M.E.

"There is no shame in not knowing; the shame lies in not finding out." – Russian Proverb

Before ripping off our Fig Leaves, let's face S.H.A.M.E. head on! Instead of hiding behind it you will be using it as a guide to learn some practical and fun ways to get to know each better. Discussion and discovery exercises following each letter in the word will help to draw you closer to each other.

S – **Share**
H – **Have Fun**
A – **Accept and Adjust**
M – **Make Changes & Mirror**
E – **Express Love**

S.H.A.M.E.

S̲.H.A.M.E.
S is for Sharing

Open and honest sharing is the foundation of this entire book and the bedrock of successful relationships. Both partners are responsible for creating a Safe Haven in which to share without risk of exposure or being judged.

Our Fig Leaves cover some amazing things. The topics range from life altering and emotionally challenging topics like abortion, past relationships, mental and physical abuse, and sexual fantasies and desires to the more mundane like pre-marital debt, poor career choices, medical issues, and so on. Is there anything you feel shameful about? Have you discussed this with your partner?

No Fig Leaves Allowed!

Sharing and getting things out in the open may be stressful but it can also be cathartic. It can lend context to how individuals react to each other and to their environment. By sharing the truth a husband can be much more understanding of his wife if, for instance, he knew why she felt uncomfortable when she was touched a certain way. Likewise, a wife can be far more empathetic if she understood why, for example, her husband seems so obsessive about money.

Any progress towards knocking down the barriers to fruitful relationships must begin with sharing thoughts and feelings with each other. New grooms and brides, for instance, invariably bring their own closets full of fashionable Fig Leaves to their honeymoon and beyond, never realizing how potentially harmful they can be. The same can be said for just about any other personal relationship.

During the process of learning or sharing the naked truth feelings can be hurt and anger can develop. There might also be myriad other feelings accompanied by negative thoughts and the impulses to act on them. These feelings are normal and not to be feared. They must, however, be dealt with constructively if a relationship is to flourish. Taking the time to share your feelings is vital but it must be done deliberately and with purpose. As Dr. Patrick Malone remarked in his book, *The Art of Intimacy*, "Intimacy is the most meaningful and courageous of all human experiences." So remember, you're not sharing for sharing's sake. You share to learn about each other and make your relationship grow. You share to promote intimacy.

Sharing time is only for sharing

Sharing time is not for arguing, accusing, yelling, sarcasm, or placing blame. Rather, it is a time to share and, in turn, listen. Gaining insight and understanding is your goal.

Discovery 3:
Get Naked!

Consider your and your partner's answers to the following questions:

When you heard *"Get Naked!"* what came to mind?

- **Did you automatically think of sex?**

- **Were you aroused or did you get a feeling of obligation?**

- **Did you feel vulnerable or embarrassed to think or speak about it at all?**

- **Do you feel safe sharing your feelings and issues with your partner now? Why, or why not?**

- **How do you think life and relationships would differ if you could openly say what you thought and felt without judgment or risk?**

- **How did your partner's answers differ from yours?**

No Fig Leaves Allowed!

YOUR NOTES

"Getting Naked!" evokes different thoughts and emotions to different people. Whether referring to physical or figurative nakedness, we must constantly balance the benefits of disclosure with the vulnerabilities of exposure. For *The "No Fig Leaves Allowed!" Approach* to work, nakedness needs to be agreed to and mutually committed to by both parties in the relationship. Only then can risk be mitigated to the point where you can *Get Naked!* without fear.

If you are in a relationship with someone who is not interested in creating a safe place where both of you can disclose your most intimate thoughts and feelings then you may need to seek professional counseling. Absent, the commitment for you both to *Get Naked!, The "No Fig Leaves Allowed!" Approach* may not work. You must discard emotional inhibitions with each other.

Our inhibitions can lead to self-consciousness and an inability to relax and be genuine within our relationships. Understanding the source of those inhibitions can be liberating and help you find a path to each other so you can enjoy your relationship fully and intimately.

Our past offers insight into our relationships' present and future. If left without examination or review, we live with a false security at best and with a ticking time bomb at worst. Without understanding our past, the best we can hope to achieve is survival of the daily grind. You cannot expect your partner to understand your needs or expectations if there is no frame of reference. You need to paint the picture. The *"No Fig Leaves Allowed!" Approach* is your paintbrush.

Examining the past and how it shapes your emotions can help lift the yoke of unresolved internal conflict and thereby preclude it from tarnishing the joy that can be found in the intimate relationship we seek. Understanding your past might also lend some insight into why you felt the way you did when first you heard *"Get Naked!"*

Before digging deep into your emotions it is vital to recognize that memories shape the way you react to the challenges of a relationship and will can bind you from fully giving and receiving love. Memories can keep you from *"Getting Naked!"* Understanding your past can help you better understand why you feel, act, and react the way you do. Embrace your past and share it. Seek emotional nakedness with yourself and your current or future partner.

If you truly value your relationship you must discard all inhibitions. Openness and honesty is vital if a relationship is to not just survive, but thrive. Are you willing to **get over yourself and move forward in your relationship? Is your partner?** There is no room for hang-ups and excuses. **You have to communicate openly and honestly.**

"Walk openly and unashamed"

As embarrassing or painful as sharing can be, being open, unguarded, and willing to listen to and accept criticism is a vital component of this journey. If you are truly dedicated to honest and healthy relationships you must **work towards strengthening and improving communication without barriers or resentment.** Understanding your naked-self empowers you to walk openly and unashamed of who you are and sets your relationship up for true fulfillment.

Sharing your true feelings without risk of coming under attack or the need to become defensive might be a little uncomfortable or embarrassing but is nevertheless liberating. The sharer's good intentions, however, must never be doubted and **the message must always be delivered with love and compassion.** Anything else will lead to conflict and misunderstanding.

Make it your goal to create a Safe Haven together and cherish the unobstructed view of each other's true self. Your relationship is meant to be a safe and beautiful place. It is meant to be free of judgment and criticism. It is meant to be a place where you can *Get Naked!* and be free to explore each other.

A Safe Haven is a relationship where two or more people can interact openly and honestly. Once this safe place is created, committed partners must safeguard it and not allow others to enter unless they too are willing to accept open and honest interaction. This Safe Haven is where you can share your deepest troubles and concerns. It must truly be a safe place to avoid the snare of "emotional infidelity." This is the trap where sharing and confiding the intimate details of your relationship with people outside your relationship can lead to a false sense of security and blindly lead you to nurture a budding emotional attachment to someone other than your partner.

Creating a Safe Haven will take practice and effort. It will take patience. And it will take a mutual commitment to nurturing a healthy relationship. Of course, when speaking your "open mind" to others there must be a certain empathy and diplomacy to mitigate the chances of conflict. **You must also be prepared to hear and accept your partner's views of you.**

Note: Most topics you have discussed thus far, and will discuss further along, are concerned with and focused on couples and relationships. But a "relationship" can include any number of people and combinations of interpersonal connections whether married or single, parent to child, co-workers, etc.

DISCOVERY 4:
WHAT DOES "SAFE HAVEN" MEAN TO YOU?

Some points to ponder:

If someone makes you uncomfortable in a relationship, would you continue to spend a lot of time with that person?

If someone or some behavior makes your partner (husband, wife, friend, etc.) uncomfortable, would you continue to associate with that person or engage in that behavior at the risk of your treasured relationship?

Do you currently have friends, family, or circumstances you believe are a threat to a valued relationship?

Are insecurities a threat to your relationship with someone special?

Do you feel comfortable and safe enough to show your true self to those whom you value?

Are you trustworthy enough to allow those you value to feel comfortable and safe enough to show their true selves to you?

"Being honest may not get you a lot of friends, but it'll get you the right ones . . ." — John Lennon

In a Safe Haven you can be real and those around you can be real with you. In a Safe Haven, there are *"No Fig Leaves Allowed!"*

In the crazy vortex of Fig Leaves we live in, people often become preoccupied with pleasing others at any cost. It's a surefire way of denying yourself the joy of inner peace and self-acceptance.

Let's consider a play on the Golden Rule that beckons us all to do unto others, as we would like done unto us. When it comes to relationships it is often the case that how we do unto others is a direct reflection of how we feel about ourselves, or perhaps how others have done unto us. It is a reactive approach to relationships rather than a proactive one. For a relationship to thrive the paradigm has to be shifted from reactive to proactive. This is only possible through open and honest communication framed by a clear understanding of how the past affects the present.

"Always speak the truth"

Real Friends Get Real!

"Getting Naked!" with everyone in your world might be a slow transition. You don't need to streak through life demanding all take notice of your new Nakedness. Not everyone is ready for that flash of reality. Remember though, your goal is to let them "see you naked" so they know you value them enough to always speak the truth. Initially you may find your circle of true friends and trustworthy people is quite a bit smaller than you thought. *That's OK. "You got the right ones, baby!"*

Ultimately, *"Getting Naked!"* is about cultivating your close personal relationships. It is about surrounding yourself with only those people who are truthful, trustworthy, supportive, and naked with you. It's about creating a Safe Haven where you can

communicate openly and honestly about anything. Messages are sent and received with a confidence that comes from a deep understanding of what makes each of you tick. You must be able to listen and accept each other's point of view. Be sensitive to each other's feelings and predispositions to certain emotions or hot topics. Again, the goal here is to **speak your heart and mind without risk.**

While discovering each other, try to remember that in a Safe Haven feelings are not wrong! Misunderstandings, preconceived notions, or a lack of trust can influence or mislead our reactions to events or issues, but our feelings about them are neither right nor wrong. We all have a right to embrace, explore, and to understand where they came from and to be able to put them in perspective. Be careful to not ascribe meaning or faults based on feelings alone since often times they are not founded on facts but misperceptions, experiences from our own past, or just the wrong information.

You also have a responsibility to identify the source(s) of your feelings while accepting that you are in control. Your feelings cannot linger or consume you if you don't let them. While keeping control of your feelings, you must acknowledge the fact your partner's feelings are not yours, but hers alone. You cannot define your partner's feelings any more than your partner can

No Fig Leaves Allowed!

define yours. For instance, telling your husband he is full of hate infers he lacks emotional control. An emotional attack like that sets the scene for barriers to build and often prevents reasonable, effective communication from blossoming. Any hope of connecting or rebuilding might evaporate quickly or seem a lost cause. If, on the other hand, you patiently and persistently apply the *"No Fig Leaves Allowed!" Approach* in a concerted effort to understand the feeling and learn why it occurred, you might find that your empathy will go a long way in building trust and strengthening the foundations of your Safe Haven. As you build your Safe Haven you may notice that the intensity and frequency of negative reactions become less frequent.

How feelings are communicated, however, does matter. Sometimes it helps to talk about feelings in the 3rd person to get it out for objective discussion. Calling the feeling a name, such as shyness, anger, fear, or any other number of names might be useful. When a feeling is labeled as something that transcends the person, it might be easier to talk about

> *"Seek first to understand, then be understood"*

it. Ultimately, however, it is the sender's responsibility to ensure the message sent is honest and clear. Likewise, it is the recipient's responsibility to empathize in an effort to ensure the message sent was indeed the message received. As renowned author and businessman Dr. Stephen Covey wrote in *The Seven Habits of Highly Effective People*, **"Seek first to understand, then to be understood."**

Don't fake it 'till you make it!

Covering the truth or faking concerns or feelings about anything will not move a relationship in a positive direction. Many of us avoid the hard truths as a way to avoid confrontation. Acting on impulse, the whim of others, or speaking according to others'

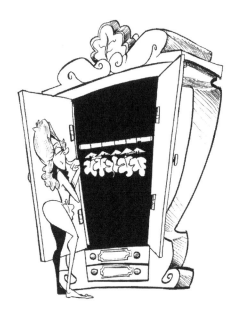

expectations is not an option. **Only the truth will do.**

Aim to please but wisely choose whom to please. Though most of us innately want to please ourselves, many of us want to please others as well. Seldom does anyone want to be seen as a failure or disappoint those we care about. We want to be informed and be on top of all the world expects of us. We want to meet expectations.

If you buy into the world's expectations and frame your self-worth by the value others place on you, disappointment is sure to follow. How can you possibly measure up? Your doubts will give rise to insecurities and add to your wardrobe of Fig Leaves. You hide behind an image created for you. You cover your true self for the sake of appearances but the more you cover up the more vulnerable your relationship is. Not being 100% honest is an unfair proposition for any relationship and it's not fertile ground for love and affection. Don't bite into that apple. Don't put on those Fig Leaves. *Get Naked!*

Once you reach your naked state it may be tempting to encourage others to join you. Not everyone is ready or willing to do so. This is awkward if you have had "friends" for years that may no longer be "welcome" or fit in your life. Rather than pushing them or ripping off their Fig Leaves, lead by example.

It is essential you remain committed to moving your relationship or friendship forward towards complete emotional nakedness. If you feel insecure about anything discuss your insecurities before hidden issues poison your relationship. This is where many couples just give up and claim irreconcilable differences. The good news is this can also be a new beginning!

Leaf by Leaf

This next discovery is as revealing as you are willing to make it. I encourage you to answer each question with candor in an effort to reveal your true self as an individual and as partners. Peel off the Fig Leaves and shed the pretenses that often lead to superficial relationships.

Caution: This next discovery may bring some serious concerns to the surface that perhaps one or both of you felt uncomfortable sharing in the past. Be empathetic as some answers may be just as difficult to hear, as they are to share.

As you complete the next discovery be sensitive to the fact that seemingly insignificant things might add up to unbearable issues. These are the things that may elicit an "out of the blue" response. Be sensitive. Remember, your goal is to grow closer together by openly discussing things in a way that can only be done by being completely naked in your relationship.

This is not the time to get offended, place blame, or be embarrassed. This is time to **speak the truth in love** and gain a deep understanding of each other. You may not love the faults or issues, but don't forget, you value the person.

NOTES

Discovery 5:
Do You See What I See?

This may take some time and might not be completed in one session as you both discuss your answers and how you feel about them. Consider each answer and comment as it is derived from your hearts. Then you can work together to resolve anything that comes up.

Directions:

In the following tables score each of the traits from Zero to Four. A Zero means "I Hate It!" and a Four means "I Love It!" Rank each trait based on how you see yourself and how you see your partner.

Once you have completed BOTH columns pertaining to you, share your answers with your partner. Write the answers he/she gives you in the "You See Me" column so you can compare answers. Discuss reasons on the Notes pages that follow.

Do You See What I See?

0= Hate It; 1= Needs Work; 2= OK; 3= Satisfied; 4= Love It

Area	I See Me	I See You	You See Me
PHYSICAL			
Body			
Teeth/Breath			
Weight			
Health			
SOCIAL			
Personality			
Conversation Ability			
Past Relationship			
Facebook Friends			
Pet Peeves			
EMOTIONAL			
Conflict			
Affection			
Sexuality			
Trust			
PROFESSIONAL			
Ambition			
Education			
Time Management			
Balance Work/Home			
RELATIONAL			
Commitment			
Romantic Effort			
Communication			
Physical/Emotional			
Availability			
HABITUAL			
Drinking/Alcohol Abuse			
Smoking/Tobacco			
Partying			
Spending			

No Fig Leaves Allowed!

YOUR NOTES

YOUR PARTNER'S NOTES

No Fig Leaves Allowed!

If you both were honest in your answers you probably have been in discussion mode for a while. The naked truth is something couples often consciously or unconsciously avoid.

Once you see each other in the naked light of full disclosure don't be too tough on yourselves. Perhaps you discovered some things you are not happy with. If your partner had a hand in revealing that to you it can be a bit uncomfortable or embarrassing. You may be frustrated and tempted to put those leaves back on – Don't do it!

Resist the temptation!!!

The answers derived from this activity may have surprised you. Your feelings can and do change throughout the years and how you feel about each other is influenced by varied circumstances and shared history.

You may feel like you got the ole' bait and switch. In reality, **we are all growing and changing.** This does not necessarily mean we have to grow apart. We can choose to grow closer together.

What seemed charming early in a relationship might seem suffocating or needy later on. If your partner does not share your perception, he may not understand your need for more space now. Your partner may not have any idea why you are so turned off when all he wants is to spend every waking moment with you. The distance can grow incrementally until there is a chasm too wide to cross.

Reflection

What specific ideas and perspectives about life, people, and relationships have changed for you over the past 10 years? Write them down overleaf and share them with your partner:

YOUR NOTES

No Fig Leaves Allowed!

Once you think you have it all figured out, the scenario changes yet again; you mature, grow a family, change life goals, and age. Nothing remains constant.

That is precisely why learning to use *The "No Fig Leaves Allowed!" Approach* is so important. Once you get used to 100% honesty there will be no surprises; only minor adjustments to the sails will be needed as life's winds begin to shift.

"Commit to being the best you can be"

The main thing is to feel comfortable knowing there may be issues you need to manage, conquer, or redirect. There are many proverbial "forks in the road." Some seem to occur in the moment-by-moment while others are a bit more long-term.

Creating an awareness of these inflections in a relationship will serve to build confidence in the love and commitment being invested by you both. It will also serve to help you decide together how you can make your relationship a Safe Haven where you can grow as individuals and as a couple.

Choose to discover and embrace the changes as opportunities to regenerate your relationship and seek every opportunity to please and **lift each other up**.

The apples of temptation can fool couples into wearing Fig Leaves and acting like all is well in an effort to cover the deficiencies in their relationships. Removing those Fig Leaves is healthy and necessary if the relationship is to thrive.

Sadly, the majority of us are so accustomed to wearing Fig Leaves it simply seems natural. We tend to be all too willing to eat society's apples and let the seeds of discord take root in our relationships until one day we feel we don't know each other anymore. We may think we don't really care to know each other anymore either. We become indifferent.

When partners in a relationship get to the point of ambivalence or despair they are unlikely to see a path back to each other. Simply "hanging in there" is no longer a viable choice because the mountain of resentment seems too tall to climb.

The lines between right and wrong, and between what is acceptable and what is not acceptable, begins to blur until both partners abandon their commitment to each other and begin living separate lives in their thoughts, in their hearts, and ultimately, in their deeds. This is when they likely and often, decide to terminate the relationship.

For some relationships, the end may or may not be complete separation. Many couples are together in name or function only. Their knots are tied by obligation and expectation but they no longer walk their paths together.

Countless couples accept and endure lifeless, loveless relationships. They see it as their new normal. That is a foundation for a miserable existence. Everyone deserves better.

And so the rocky journey continues as long as both men and women still believe Fig Leaves will cover up their insecurities and forays into temptation. In the process they will collect a wardrobe of Fig Leaves as they go so deep undercover from their true selves they can no longer recognize true love.

"You may find yourself an 'empty vessel'"

Relationship failure is rampant, almost expected by many, and occurs often because the truth was never revealed in the beginning or has been repeatedly suppressed along the way. We are so used to wearing Fig Leaves that we no longer notice we're wearing them or how to relate to our partner.

Warning: Your partner may not be whom you think (or remember).

Some folks do have serious unresolved issues. Building a relationship with them will not come without challenges and often happens with many red flags waving. Not seeing the red flag might be a function of a good cover up. As an active participant in a relationship you have a responsibility to know and make sure you are committing to the person you think you are committing to and for revealing your true self as well.

While you are in the whirlwind of romance sometimes issues are overlooked entirely and little time is spent figuring out how they may impact your relationship in the future. This isn't necessarily done out of ignorance. It is very possible to be blinded by emotional moments and focus only on what you like about people. Effective, honest, and objective communication is key!

There may come times in relationships where short bursts of nurturing and giving by only one partner is necessary to overcome a challenging period, or later in life, as changing circumstances and declining health dictate. Ultimately, if the foundation of nakedness is there you will be able to stabilize the relationship through compassionate discussion.

Sometimes life presents us with challenges. Being a partner to someone in crisis requires extreme selflessness, but often results in an inequitable relationship. You need to find balance. If balance cannot be restored because of a selfish partner, the relationship will head in a negative direction.

Outside of health issues or accidents, hanging on to a one sided relationship is not healthy. At some point you will need to make the decision whether you will continue in an empty, unfulfilling, one sided relationship or move on without your partner. Either decision can be made in peace knowing that you did all you could to be honest and true to your own feelings. In these instances it's key is to surround yourself with friends and depend on a safe support system.

By getting emotionally naked, communicating, and working on the relationship, both participants will be rewarded with a deep love and understanding that could never be experienced with another otherwise. The history shared makes success that much sweeter and the love that much greater.

"The grass ain't greener on the 'other side', the grass ain't greener on your side. It's greener where you water it." — *Robert Fulghum*

Starting over may seem like a great idea on the surface. Sad and alone are those who made the decision to end a relationship prematurely instead of communicating and fighting for what they valued. They will live with regret and a lifetime of "what-ifs" knowing they didn't give it their best shot.

"The grass isn't greener because it is better over there, it is greener because it is over a septic tank." — *Erma Bombeck*

Impulsively, and in the short term, starting over can seem like a relief. But if the underlying issues remain unresolved any new relationship is bound to turn into yet another roller-coaster ride. Life becomes a succession of first-dates where there are no real expectations. This is true for many of the serial nuptial or intimacy seekers. That can be exciting on the front-end for sure, but for those afraid to get emotionally naked it is ultimately unfulfilling and cowardly.

Of course, with experience comes experience. Some folks who have married more than once do learn the lessons and have gone on to have successful relationships. Unfortunately, much damage has been done, years and fortunes lost, and relationships destroyed or estranged, as those journeys unfold and lessons are learned. Hopefully, in learning about each other you can avoid the damaging effects of unfulfilled relationships and painful breakups.

What are the signs?

Focusing only on who we think we *should be* and trying to meet others' expectations are Fig Leaves that separate us from those to whom we want to be close.

Unable to stand emotionally naked in front of each other, couples may be sexually inhibited and thereby experience an unfulfilling physical relationship as well. Because they are "wearing Fig Leaves" sex becomes an awkward act rather than a joyful experience.

Meanwhile, the withering relationship continues with one person usually doing more of the giving or more of the taking. Eventually both participants may end up feeling used, empty, or completely dissatisfied. Naturally, they start to drift apart and one or both will feel that sharing themselves physically or emotionally is shameful or futile. No longer will the couple stand there, naked without shame. Rather, the "lights go out" and emotional and physical intimacy are left in the dark. Many times, this leads to one or both partners seeking solace in a distraction, perhaps with someone or something outside the relationship. This can be a co-worker, an old flame, neighbor, even a stranger or a vice. This is very self-deceiving and damaging to a committed relationship.

Feelings and fears often serve to create distance between you and your partner. When a couple has distance between them and indifference sets in, the road to reconciliation is long. It may be long, but it's not impossible if you both listen emphatically and empathetically to each other. Do not judge. Always remember that feelings are not wrong and never forget to have a little fun along the way.

No Fig Leaves Allowed!

S.<u>H</u>.A.M.E.
H is for Having Fun

This may seem very basic. After all, many relationships begin with a flirty look, a fun date, and a whirlwind courtship. Circumstances, age, health issues, emotional baggage, schedules, children, and myriad other life happenings will take their toll. Don't allow emotional apathy to sneak up and steal your fun.

There are also other couples that don't start their relationship with fun and frolic but must learn as they go and grow. It doesn't matter which category you find yourself in, you must make time for some lighthearted laughter. If you are bored in your relationship, maybe it's because you're boring. Maybe your partner is boring. Consider going back to the beginning – "back to basics" as the saying goes. Think about the things you did when you first got together and try some of those again. You might find that it spices things up a bit or you might find that you have grown and actually have new interests you can explore together.

Realize too that you and your partner may be on different schedules and moods. You, or your partner, might also be experiencing hormonal changes, physical challenges, or stress. Those are all barriers to intimacy that must be acknowledged and addressed. You both must be creative at times and inject the element of fun whenever possible.

Individuals must not rely on others for happiness. **Create your own happiness** until the opportunity to share it opens.

Think of it as a card game. You can play many rounds of solitaire until someone shows up to play poker.

Remember U is the center of F U N!

Say it out loud, **"I am Fun! We are Fun! Let's have Fun!"**

In a relationship, partners may have their own hobbies or ideas about what is fun to do. One may enjoy sailing, thrill rides, and training for triathlons. The other might enjoy relaxing dinners, dancing, basking in the sun on the beach, or strolling through an art fair or flea market hunting for treasures. There's

"Create your own happiness"

nothing wrong with that. Enjoy your individual pursuits, but find ways to combine activities so both of you are fulfilled. Find new things to do together too. It is important to learn to enjoy seeing each other as an individual and sharing in each other's joy.

To balance individual alone time and space, which is important, continually seek new activities and experiences you both enjoy. Cooperation is crucial. When pleasing each other is priority number one, it may surprise you to find fun in activities you wouldn't normally enjoy.

Many couples are fortunate to have the same interests and can spend every winter on the slopes together or camping every summer. The key point here is to **find some fun activities you are willing to do together** and also give each other plenty of opportunities and space to take time alone, or with friends, to pursue individual interests.

If riding a bike together on a busy road doesn't suit one partner, then perhaps a ride together on the beach can satisfy both. Perhaps one partner can help the other fulfill a dream or interest and then cheer them on! The support shown here will pay dividends and elicit equal support for the other partner's interests. In the process, new interests surface and common memories are likely to be made.

It can also be especially gratifying and revitalizing to pick up an activity that you used to share in the early, exciting days of a relationship.

My husband and I met on the dance floor. Dancing and music have always been a huge part of who I am. He fell in love with that. Over the years, we have tried to keep the excitement of our first connection by going dancing. Careers, kids, and life have definitely created obstacles. It has been challenging at times. Staying committed, getting creative with our couple time, and making an effort to get back in step with each other, has proven to work every time.

When you have totally different interests that seem to keep you apart for the majority of your free time, it might be time to discover some new things you can enjoy together. If your time together is limited, search for and use even the smallest opportunities to spend quality time together. There is no room for selfishness if the goal is a healthy connection. Make it a priority.

"Spend quality time together"

There are numerous activities to enforce your new Mandatory Fun policy that will help build a healthy relationship. A quick internet search will give you a list of anything from zip lining for a fresh sex life, to sweating it out at the gym, to signing up for a cooking class. You both must have the freedom to share your thoughts and feelings about the current state of your fun-o-meter and commit to having some fun.

No Fig Leaves Allowed!

Discovery 6:
Are You Having Fun?

What to do, What to do . . .

How would you describe the fun in your relationship?

List some specific fun things / hobbies you
like to do:

In the space below, list some specific fun
things/hobbies your partner likes to do:

Hobbies to start or share together:

Enjoy reading & highlighting some of these suggestions for couple activities:

- Learn to play a sport. Tennis, racquetball, golf, etc.

- Buy bikes and start riding to breakfast on weekends.

- Sign up for a Yoga or Zumba class.

- Learn to surf.

- Get a personal trainer and train for an event or contest.

- Take up bird watching. Go on hikes to identify.

- Join a gym. Go together.

- Go sailing / learn to sail.

- Join a bowling league.

- Join an outdoor adventure club.

- Start a monthly Dinner Date Club with friends.

- Take some college electives.

- Go for a walk together.

- Fly a kite.

- Go to a stationary store and read greeting cards to each other.

- Play I-Spy.

No Fig Leaves Allowed!

- Pick a cookbook and find a new recipe to try.

- Create artwork together. Frame & hang it in your home or office.

- Take a shower together and don't speak at all.

- Go dancing or join a Ballroom Dance class together.

- Get paper and crayons, play some music, and "draw" to the music. Do this on separate paper or together.

- Go to the beach and build a sand castle.

- Take turns giving each other a massage.

- Get a couple's massage.

- Plant flowers or edible plants in a garden or in a pot.

- Get fresh ingredients and make smoothies.

- Play arcade games.

- Locate volunteer work you can do together.

- Return together to where you first met.

- Do some research and compile your family trees.

- Take a class together about something neither knows anything about.

- Take your clothes off and paint each other's bodies.

- Read poetry to each other.

- Write poetry about each other.

- Get a book you both want to read and take turns reading it aloud at night before bed.

- Go to a carnival & play all the games.

- Find a roller-coaster and go for a ride.

- Go to the beach for a picnic.

- Go for a bike ride.

- Ride a motorcycle together.

- Pack an overnight bag. Go to airport. Buy tickets for a flight . . . anywhere.

- Go on a cruise!

- Get lost in a maze & find your way back to each other.

- Go to a comedy club.

- Take boudoir photos of each other . . . *GET NAKED!* — *Really* Naked.

Pick one of these activities to do at least once a week!

Other ideas:

No Fig Leaves Allowed!

S.H.A.M.E.
A is for Acceptance
& Adjustment

You might have come across some issues or learned new aspects about your partner through the previous exercises that you don't quite know what to do with or how to feel about. Just because you did not know these things does not mean that what you do know of your partner is of any less value.

Full disclosure can be difficult for some people and can be embarrassing, depressing, or even painful. This is especially true as someone you love recounts a difficult experience or shares his or her heart with you. You need to decide whether your relationship and the person you love are worth making a genuine effort to overcome the discomfort. Will you accept the whole person with her mistakes, insecurities, and vulnerabilities? By creating a Safe Haven for sharing your feelings, you **minimize feelings of exposure while encouraging disclosure.**

"The past is not a weapon"

Can you accept mistakes were made, harsh words may have been said, and feelings may have been hurt?

Can you accept hearing you may not have been providing the affection needed?

Can you make amends and make your way back towards each other?

Can you move on?

The information shared can be just as difficult to hear, as it is to say. As a sender, you need to accept that you may experience a negative reaction to your message as well. As a receiver, you need to understand that whatever was told to you may have been so difficult to say that your partner did not know how or if to tell you. This is true for folks who would rather avoid confrontations of any kind. It is risky to share in any case, but even more so when a partner's reaction is unpredictable or predictably adverse. There may be guilt or other emotions tied to sharing that will need to be discussed as well, but getting things in the open is the foundation of a strong relationship.

At this point, there is no need to discuss the reason why you were not told something earlier. The past is only serving as a portal of information to help you understand each other and grow closer. The trajectory is forward. The past is not to be dragged into every conversation. It is not to be used as a weapon to hurt each other.

Once you have this information about your partner or yourself, you may need to make certain adjustments to your relationship boundaries, lifestyle, and how you relate each other.

You need to accept your partner, as you would hope he or she would accept you.

"Accept your partner"

As you move forward together, continue employing *The "No Fig Leaves Allowed!" Approach*. When either of you believe the other is not fully emotionally naked, say so! Just lovingly say, **"No Fig Leaves Allowed! Now tell me what is bothering you."** This phrase should place you in your Safe Haven for honest communication. There is no judgment or threat, no name-calling or anger. It is just sharing. How can you know your partner's needs or expect your needs to be met, if you do not convey them to each other? You can't. **You both have a responsibility to communicate honestly.**

It is tough enough to meet someone that will tell you when you have food in your teeth! It is rare to find someone to always tell you the truth. When you find that person, you have found a treasure; someone you can share your life with. Be that someone. This is why giving this book to all of your single friends is such a crazy-smart idea. What a way to start a relationship!

Most of us want to be accepted. Some of us expect to be accepted just as we are, completely covered in Fig Leaves with no hope of disrobing. Excuses abound: "I'm just set in my ways," or, "I've always done things this way," or even, "My last partner couldn't accept me." These are not the words of an emotionally naked

"We are constantly changing"

person who values a relationship. This is the voice of a selfish and emotionally lazy person who is completely focused on self. **The truth is we are all constantly changing and we can all make adjustments in our relationships.** You should never be happy standing still in life or in relationship with a stagnant person.

You can't demand what you can't provide. —Jocolbia Johnson

Discovery 7:
Where There's a Will
There's An 'A'

Read through and write some of the things you discovered during previous exercise about yourself and your partner that will require you to be accepting. What adjustments will you need to make to move your relationship forward in a positive trajectory?

Examples:

Accept: We are not perfect.
Adjust: Be quick to apologize.

Accept: We will not forget.
Adjust: Be willing to move forward.

Accept: We cannot change the past.
Adjust: Learn from the past to understand your present.

Accept: Changing how we feel & act may take some time.
Adjust: Acknowledge & celebrate small successes.

Accept: We will get frustrated.
Adjust: Stay couple centric and motivated!

Accept: Our relationship requires emotional investment. I'm not the "mushy" type.
Adjust: Get over it and *Get Naked!*

No Fig Leaves Allowed!

Your turn:

Accept:

Adjust:

Accept:

Adjust:

Accept:

Adjust:

Accept:

Adjust:

Accept:

Adjust:

Accept:

Adjust:

Accept:

Adjust:

No Fig Leaves Allowed!

S.H.A.<u>M</u>.E.
M IS FOR MIRRORING &
MAKING CHANGES

"We can't solve problems by using the same kind of thinking we used when we created them." — Albert Einstein

Once we find discrepancies in how we view our partner and ourselves and compare them with how we relate to each other, changes may be in order. These may be small changes or real big ones. Some we may be able to apply right away and others may take months to take root. **Though you can influence your partner, you can only do your part** to make things right in a relationship. If you are in a relationship but are reading this book alone and your partner has no interest in participating, you may have a long haul.

"You can only do your part"

There may come a point when you decide to lay it out and ask your partner if he feels you and the relationship are important enough to make the effort. The answer – or lack of one – will speak volumes and no doubt spawn a very interesting discussion . . . **that could be a great start, a finish, or a new beginning**.

Many relationships grow around hurt feelings or spiritual wounds. These may run deeper than we realize. These may drive partners to behave in certain ways and even elicit a negative response to a positive stimulus. Couples may be so fearful of trusting one another that they unconsciously distance themselves emotionally. If emotions are negative and trust is on the wane of non-existent, physical intimacy is close behind or already gone.

We may look for shreds of doubt in the most innocent of acts. If we all scrutinize our partners closely enough we will find fault and we will all be caught in moments of distance or weakness. The mistakes often made are collecting these moments over time without discussion, allowing them to define our reality, shape our perceptions, and ultimately to destroy the relationship.

> *"Don't allow 'moments of distance' to define your reality"*

It is a sad truth that the world and tabloids are chock full of broken hearts and bouts of infidelity. The reality is that the day-to-day is far from the fairytale mindset of Hollywood or young lovers. What you can do is change the way you act and react while staying true to your own feelings. You must feel it to be a worthy effort. **A relationship is a constant flow of giving and growing.** A couple must be so transparently naked with each other that un-met needs and hurts are openly discussed and addressed before seeking satisfaction outside the relationship.

If your partner has a broken heart or her soul is suffering, you are the caretaker, not the judge. What may seem insignificant to you can be devastating to your partner based on life experiences. If the past is prologue then understanding the past will help you build your relationship on solid ground. If you find the barriers of the past to be insurmountable then this might be a good time to seek the wise counsel of a professional therapist. You may find the investment well worth your time and expense.

YOUR NOTES

Discovery 8:
Reflection & Application

Reflection

Take a moment and think about your past relationships and experiences. Is it possible your emotional wounds and scars are affecting your current relationship? Can you recall particularly challenging events or difficult people that may have contributed to your perspective on various situations? List any life changing experiences, trials, or disappointments that may be impacting your relationship today.

_____

_____

_____

_____

_____

_____

_____

Use the NOTES page at the end of this section if you need to list more.

No Fig Leaves Allowed!

Application

Revisit your shared answers for Discovery 2 (The Comfort Meter). Identify Hot Topics you feel or believe are related to the emotional experiences on the previous page.

Do any of these apply to challenges you are currently facing today? Share them with your partner. Apply *The "No Fig Leaves Allowed!" Approach* to help each other understand the root of your true feelings. Consider viewing these, and all challenges, as riddles to be solved together regardless of where they stem from. This can help refocus the attention on resolution instead of entering a cycle of arguing and blame. Clearly articulate your needs and feelings but avoid projecting your past anger or disappointments upon your partner. If possible, resolve your pain with the one who caused you suffering. Carrying pain and disdain from any other time in your life into your relationship is called baggage, and there's no room for that in your sanctuary. It's important to remain in the present while understanding the past events that may be driving your reactions and emotions. Decide to overcome. Don't let a past failure or disappointment steal your joy today.

Something to ponder . . .

You will always find points of conflict in any relationship. Some are so common that they've become humorous clichés; put the toilet seat down, make the bed, the thermostat – she likes it hot, he likes it cold, football Sunday and the poor sports widows, the trip to the mall, and on and on. And those are the easy ones.

Some are far more complex; finances, sex, and big decisions, like buying a house, a career change, or how to discipline a child. Each can be a spark to an argument or it can be an opportunity to objectively approach resolution. It's a choice, and the choice is yours.

No Fig Leaves Allowed!

YOUR NOTES

Discovery 9:
Mirror, Mirror

Mirror, mirror what do you see? In the popular fairytale Snow White, the Evil Queen spent hours in front of the magic mirror obsessed with the answer to her daily question: "Who is the fairest of them all?" I am definitely not a fan of her unhealthy approach to self-worth and her obsession with outward beauty. Most notably, however, the Evil Queen asked the mirror for the truth. We know how that story goes. She got the truth, but instead of improving areas that needed

No Fig Leaves Allowed!

it, she went into the world and belittled or tried to eliminate anyone that failed to meet her expectations or diminished her self-perceived stature. In the end, she could never measure up and lost everything.

In a relationship, we often ask our partners what they think about this or that. When we ask about intimate issues or concerns it is important to see yourself through your partner's eyes. Your partner, in a way, is your mirror. But you must work together to address the reflection in a way that honors both you and your relationship. Though your partner is your mirror, he is not there to define how you feel. Your feelings are your own. In serving as your mirror, however, he is there to help you understand how your feelings influence your behavior and in turn, the relationship itself. Tell your partner how you feel. Use words like, "I feel distant," "I feel like I am alone right now." "I am angry," "I feel empty," and so on.

By sharing how you feel you get things out in the open, but you also afford your partner insight into your mental state. You allow him or her to know that something is going on. With this understanding, he can offer you a reflection from a mirror framed with context. By offering up your feelings, you are opening a path to your heart.

Mirror Imaging Exercise Directions:

Stand in front of your partner and take turns sharing aloud each of the issues, Hot Topics, and Apples you discovered in previous activities. Share them one at a time by starting each phrase with "I" or "My". For example:

You:
"I feel uncomfortable talking about . . . "

Your partner:
Repeats what you say and then asks "is this what you meant."

You:

Say "yes" or "no" to confirm message sent was the message received.

You & your partner:

Share and discuss ways you both can respond to each other's needs in the future to make sure you both feel safe.

This exercise helps eliminate errors and misunderstandings and ensures your feelings are heard and taken seriously. It is each partner's responsibility to tend to the heart of the other.

"Tended hearts are tender"

If you are without a partner, stand in front of an actual mirror and document your answers. Asking yourself and confirming your willingness to make the changes necessary will be the start to a great plan for achieving emotional nakedness.

S.H.A.M.<u>E</u>.

E IS FOR EXPRESSIONS OF LOVE

In this discussion you will explore each other's view of what love looks like. How do you send and receive love? What is an accurate expression of love?

You can say "I love you" many times a day but if your actions repeatedly say "I don't care" then the message is lost in translation. What message are you sending? What is being received?

Consider this elementary school classic:
Do you like me? (Yes or No)
Do you love me? (Yes or no)

Have you have ever given or received a note like this?

Remember when as kids we wanted to know if someone liked us? We would just ask by writing a simple, concise question on our notebook paper, maybe folding it a special way, and passing it along. Then we'd get an answer and know exactly where we stood. It was innocent, perhaps, but it was effective.

You can use this note passing as a "safe" way to check the tempo of your interactions. You can also have a private dialogue in a journal. This can help cool a Hot Topic so productive conversation can proceed.

Liking and loving . . .

There may be times in your relationship when you don't like how you are being treated, how your feelings are ignored or dismissed, or how your partner's attitude in the morning starts your day all wrong. It is at those moments when you could probably answer "No" to the "Do you like me?" question.

You definitely love your partner, your family, your history, your partnership . . . but you don't really "like" them very much at the moment. It is during these times you need to be sure you both feel secure in knowing you can still answer "Yes" to the "Do you love me?" question. Your love is there. You're just in a temporary funk.

"I 'love' you but I don't 'like' you"

Feeling distant, indifferent, unappreciated, dissatisfied, or just plain annoyed, is a terrible place to be. Left unchecked or unaddressed, those feelings can lead to doubt in the value of your relationship. Does it have what it takes to be all you dreamed it could be? Can you even stand to be in the same room with your honey? Was it all a ruse? Did you ever really love each other? These are tough questions. Look beyond the doubt and you might find the love is in there, buried **under the "I don't like yous."**

You need to get back to liking each other. This is where honest communication and *The "No Fig Leaves Allowed!" Approach* can help. This is when you dig deep and ensure you both understand when needs are not being met and how they can be fulfilled. Everyone has bad days. Trials are part of every relationship. Expressing love in the midst of conflict is tough. Nevertheless, you both have a responsibility to put your relationship first, secure in your love and commitment, so a bad mood doesn't escalate into your breakfast ending up on your head.

Loving your partner and expressing love for your partner are two very different things. You must master both.

So, how do you express your love? The simple answer is "sincerely." That is to say, express your love free from pretense or deceit; proceeding from genuine feelings. What that means is ultimately up to you and your partner. Yes, you both have a vote. Love is a feeling and a flow. It is a message sent and received and like any message, it can come across as garbled.

External influences can impact how love is expressed and interpreted too. Love is often portrayed as an over-priced, over-sexed, and over-simplified emotion. The expectations are so overblown that many of us feel unlovable, inadequate, or incapable of giving or receiving sincere love.

How can anyone live up to Hollywood, billboards, porn sites, or the drama of late night TV? It's a "photoshopped" notion of love. Don't buy into it. Instead, focus on what matters most to you and your partner. Projecting false notions of love into your relationship or relying on material things as a measure of love are bound to miss the mark.

Sure, a big diamond might communicate, "I really value you." But it can also say "I'm insecure, shallow, and financially irresponsible." The *"No Fig Leaves Allowed!" Approach* can help lend some context into that message. Giving expensive material gifts as an expression of love might make sense to the one giving the

"Things cannot replace love"

gift, but when all the recipient needs or wants is a moment of listening, a tender touch, or time together, even the shiniest of trinkets loses its luster. The true needs remain un-met. The genuine sincerity is lost in translation. The gift is poorly received and, ultimately, you both remain dissatisfied. Tension grows and Fig Leaves are put on.

You both must convey your true needs while being sensitive to each other's efforts and feelings. Though fancy things can be an expression of love in the right context, things cannot replace love. Don't get confused here. Expecting things to fill in for love is shallow, unfair, and can lead to a lonely existence. We see it all the time in friends, neighbors, celebrities, politicians – people at the peak of very lucrative and powerful careers who derail themselves and their relationships through seemingly inexplicable actions. How can people who seem to have it all be so unhappy? Something is clearly missing.

Going back to Discovery 8, reflect and apply what you have learned about each other as an effort to understand what love means to each of you. Is something being lost in translation?

If your partner doesn't feel safe or doesn't understand your motivation, love cannot be fully given or received. Likewise, if you do not feel safe or fully understand your partner's motivation, you will be unable to give or receive love no matter how many shiny toys or bling you give or get.

Partners must communicate to each other using expressions of love that mean the most to each. *New York Times* bestselling author, Dr. Gary Chapman, wrote the revolutionary book, *The Five Love Languages: How to Express Heartfelt Commitment to Your Mate.* Dr. Chapman's book is a great catalyst for discussion leading to an understanding of each other's needs and the different ways those needs are met.

On his website, Dr. Chapman lists The Five Love Languages® as "Words of Affirmation, Acts of Service, Receiving Gifts, Quality Time, and Physical Touch." Which language do you think you speak? Which one does your partner speak?

As a thought exercise, choose The Love Language *you think applies to you and which one applies to your partner.* I recommend you both visit Dr. Chapman's website, www.the5lovelanguages. com. There, you can take a short survey to determine your love languages. Compare what you learned with what you thought you knew about yourself and your partner. Were you surprised?

Whether or not you agree with what you discover, reflect deeply on what you learned. It's important to know and understand. Think of it as a decoder for encrypted messages. I am confident you will find the effort insightful.

What follows is an opportunity to look into your expressions of love, how they are communicated, and how they are received.

DISCOVERY 10:
WHAT I LIKE ABOUT YOU!

How Do I Love Thee? Let Me Count The Ways

I often remind my husband I married him for his brain! I have always been impressed by how much he knows about seemingly everything. He is very well read and can maintain interesting and knowledgeable conversations with nearly anyone. I find this attractive since I enjoy a full social life and appreciate having his intellectual company to interact with our friends and the people we meet. I also enjoy his constant witty injection of clichés and colloquialisms in our everyday chatter because they keep things light and in perspective with a good boost of laughter. These are just a couple of the things I like about my dear partner in life. I try to remember to tell him often. It is important for those we love to hear the positive affirmations. It is also important to me to remember the spark that started it all.

In the "Love Notes" section below, list everything you can possibly think of that you liked or loved about your partner either when you first met or right now. In this list, include emotional, spiritual, mental, physical, relational, and sexual attributes.

When you have completed your lists (and I hope they are long), take turns sharing your thoughts with each other. If you can't come up with anything right away, think back to when you first got together. What do you remember? What was done that made you feel special or showed you how much you meant?

What were the little things that lifted you off your feet? Write those down. Share them.

Note: If you have not seen a particular trait or side of them that you love for a long time, be sure to put an asterisk next to it. Discuss.

Love Notes

DISCOVERY 11:
OUR NAKED LOVE

Sharing what you love about each other and keeping reminders of your love visible (old love notes, dancing to your song, or perusing photos of fun times and memories you share) helps liven things up. This is especially important on days when you really don't like each other much. As you learned earlier, not liking each other at times is a completely normal feeling. We all have those days. What matters most, however, is keeping focused on the value you each bring to the relationship and the investment you have made to make the relationship work.

That leads me to the final activity in this book. What follows is an unfiltered expression of your love for each other. This time it will be a tangible covenant of your feelings and a reminder of your promise to be completely naked with your thoughts and actions. Think of this as a coat of arms and standard for your own naked communication.

People often have photos of special people and experiences on their walls to remind them of good times and warm feelings. Many married folks have wedding albums or photos from their Big Day. It's important to surround yourself with reminders of the positive things in your life; the relationships you treasure, the values and virtues you consider non-negotiable, the things that really matter. What's on your walls?

Now's the time to get creative!

No Fig Leaves Allowed!

Use words, poems, pictures, shapes, glitter, and all of the supplies available to you (yes, you can use glitter) to express your hopes, dreams, and goals together. Make a collage of what matters most to you. Think of your vows, promises, and all of the discussions you have had on this journey of discovering each other.

Make it a project about honest communication. Include statements such as:

- I promise to be completely Naked with you.

- I promise to share openly about my feelings and needs.

- I promise to love you how you need to be loved.

Create your own motto like "Naked Love, Respect, Honest Communications."

Be creative. Make your own. Have fun!

When you are both done, take your works of art and share them with each other. Admire them, understand them, and embrace them. Then affix them together and frame them. Hang them on your wall. You've just created a memory and something that will always remind you that in your commitment to communicate, there are . . .

"No Fig Leaves Allowed!"

From My Heart to Yours

Dear Naked Friends,

Thank you for choosing this book to help you discover your true selves and the ability to speak out in love as you continue removing your Fig Leaves.

I commend you for trusting in yourself and your feelings for each other and hope *The "No Fig Leaves Allowed!" Approach* was helpful. Continue enjoying your newfound nakedness as you communicate with everyone in your life's path.

Now that you've had a chance to experience *The "No Fig Leaves Allowed!" Approach*, did it meet your expectations? Did you learn anything? Was it helpful? I want to know. I want to hear from you! Please share your experiences, photos, and comments and be an encouragement to others!

Join our active discussions on *Facebook @ No Fig Leaves Allowed*. Get product updates and interact with naked folks from all over the world. We all have different experiences and can learn from each other. Check us out on Twitter *@No_Fig_Leaves*. Read and retweet quotes and comments from the book to inspire others. You can also visit us on the web at *www.nofigleaves.com*. We have additional items available to keep your commitment visible and to show the world that you are Emotionally Naked and Fig Leaf free! You can also reach me anytime at *author@ nofigleaves.com*. I hope to hear from you.

Susan A. LeBron

STAY NAKED MY FRIENDS!

for ongoing support and assistance:

web: http://www.nofigleaves.com
email: author@nofigleaves.com

BIBLIOGRAPHY & SUGGESTED READING

The 5 Love Languages: The Secret to Love That Lasts, Gary D. Chapman, Dec. 2009, ISBN-13: 978-0802473158.

Love & Respect: The Love She Most Desires; The Respect He Desperately Needs, Emerson Eggerichs, 2004, ISBN-10: 1591451876.

Five ways to 'Jazz up' Your Marriage, Glen Kato, 2014, ISBN-13: 978-1633152731.

1001 Ways To Be Romantic, Gregory J.P. Godek, 5th Edition, ISBN-10: 1883518059.

30 Days to Taming Your Tongue, Deborah Smith Pegues, 2005 ISBN-13: 978-0763922104.

Love is a Decision, Gary Smalley and John Trent, 1998, ISBN-10: 0849933625.

Love'em or Lose'em, Beverly Kaye and Sharon Jordan-Evans 2nd edition, 2002, ISBN-10: 1576751406.

Shining Your Armour: The Lost Art of Romance, Gabriel Vaughn, 1992, ISBN-13: 978-0962873300.

Pretty much all of the Proverbs in the Holy Bible.

Index

Made in the USA
Charleston, SC
12 October 2014